Understanding Death & Grief

story by
David M. Lindsey, Ph.D.

illustrations and cover design by
Diane Harper

published by
Personal Growth Institute

cover painting by
Peggie Mead Koroncey

Published by:
Personal Growth Institute
2638 Browning Avenue
Lake Orion, MI 48360

ISBN 1-878040-03-0

Printed in the United States of America

Dedication

To my parents,
Arthur and Muriel Lindsey,
with love, respect and gratitude.

CHAPTER ONE

It was about eight years ago when the Wilson family moved from their apartment in the city to the quaint village of Riverside. It was a dream come true for the young family of four. They had been saving for several years to buy their first house and they had finally found exactly what they were looking for in this small, peaceful community located on the banks of the Cedar River. It wasn't a prestigious house by any means. It was just a modest, three bedroom, red brick house surrounded by fourteen acres of farmland. There was plenty of room for their family to grow and also unlimited opportunities for Buffy, their cocker spaniel puppy, to interact with nature.

Many in the community still remember Buffy's first encounter with a skunk. The offensive odor lingered in the puppy's coat for several days.

Charles Wilson considered himself to be the head of the family, even though most of the really important family decisions were made by his wife. Charlie, as his friends called him, was typical of many men in their late forties. He was concerned about the loss of his hair, the extra inches around his waist, his occasional forgetfulness and his constantly changing eyesight.

One of Charlie's most recent challenges was to accept the fact that he must wear trifocals to see correctly. It was just a few weeks ago that the doctor had given him his first pair. Charlie didn't like his new glasses and at first refused to wear them because he thought they made him look much older. But as time went by, his vanity surrendered to his better judgment. Charlie now wears his trifocals on a daily basis.

Much of the strength and integrity of the Wilson family was provided by Charlie's wife, Loretta. She was a loving, supportive woman, who also was very smart, though she usually denied it. She saw herself simply as a dedicated homemaker and part-time real estate agent, but she was much more. In fact, she was so respected by everyone in Riverside that they were going to give her a special award at the community picnic for being chairperson of the PTA.

Loretta was definitely special. She was one of those individuals who brought out the best in everyone. She loved life and approached every problem as an opportunity from God to learn and grow.

Charlie and Loretta were "blessed" with two wonderful children, although there were times when Edward and Valerie drove them up the wall. Edward was the classic example of a teenager trying to express himself in a manner that was acceptable to his peers, his parents and himself. Being a sophomore in high school was difficult for Edward, but he was determined to do the best he could.

Because of peer pressure, one never knew what to expect from Edward. Some days he would emerge from his messy room completely dressed up with every hair in place and with an overpowering scent of his father's best cologne. More often, however, his attire consisted of a black shirt with red snakes and purple lizards, wrinkled jeans that were torn at the knees, an old ball cap that was stained with perspiration, and a pair of worn-out sneakers.

Edward's younger sister, Valerie, wasn't quite yet a teenager. She was at that awkward stage in life when nothing seems to naturally fit together. Because of her rapid growth during the past year, many of her clothes appeared too short on her. This made her look even thinner than she really was, and she was quite thin.

Her slenderness, however, was just one of many things that made Val feel uncomfortable about herself. She also believed her hair was too kinky, her feet were gigantic and her smile was unattractive. Val's critical perception about herself resulted in her being very shy and, because of this, she wasn't very popular at school.

In the evenings, Val could usually be found doing homework, talking on the phone or practicing the violin. She had been taking violin lessons for the past three years but, based on the screeching sounds that came from the basement when she practiced, music was not her calling.

The day of the community picnic, the day that
Loretta had been anxiously awaiting, finally arrived. It
was on this day that she would be given an award for
her dedication to the PTA. She had never won an
award before and she was very excited and,
surprisingly, somewhat nervous. She sat down in her
oversized rocking chair, the chair that her mother had
given her, and recalled some special memories of the
past. As she sat there rocking back and forth, back
and forth, thinking about her wonderful life, the first
chest pains came.

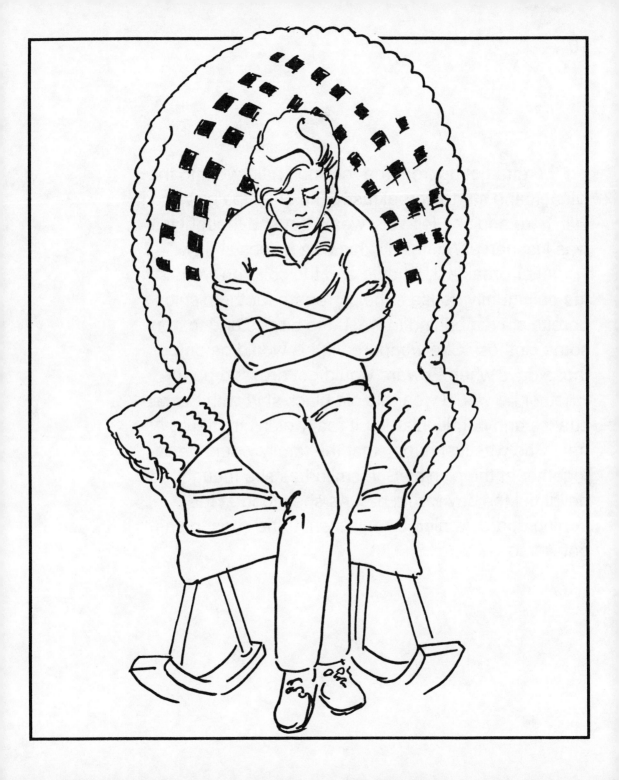

Loretta got up from the rocking chair, went to the kitchen and started breakfast. The chest pains were still there and she felt very weak, but she thought it was just nerves. After all, this was a special day.

After breakfast, Charlie and the children went to the community house to help prepare for the picnic. Loretta stayed behind to wash the dishes and to iron some clothes. She wondered if this would be one of those days when Edward would get dressed-up, or whether he would wear his old black shirt with the red snakes and purple lizards. It really didn't matter to her. She was just happy that the family would be together at the picnic. She smiled as she thought how delightful the day would be. As she stood at the ironing board, ironing Charlie's shirt, the chest pains got worse.

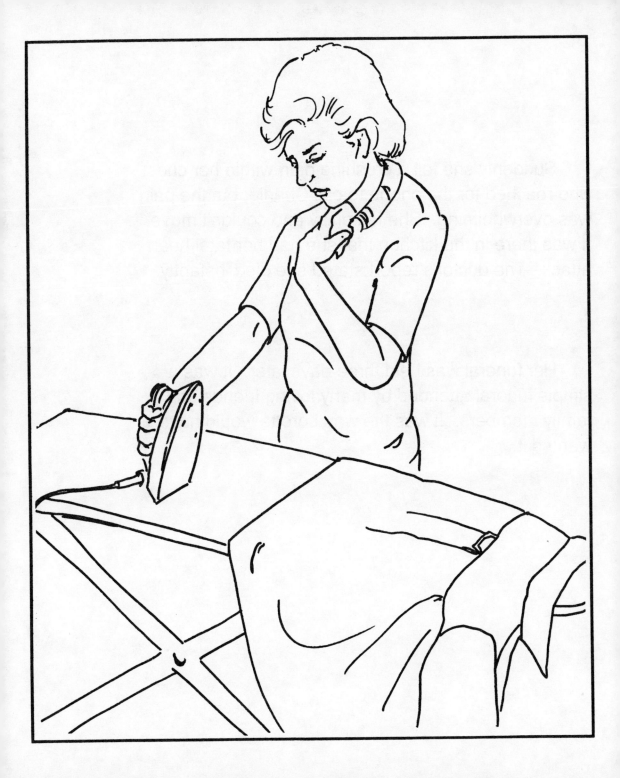

Suddenly she felt a crushing pain within her chest. She reached for the phone to call Charlie, but the pain was overwhelming. She felt dizzy and couldn't move. It was there in the kitchen that she had her fatal heart attack. The doctor's report stated she died instantly.

Her funeral was held three days later. It was a simple funeral attended by many loving friends and family members. It was the way Loretta would have wanted it.

During the next few months, Charlie, Ed and Val did the best they could to deal with their grief, but the pain was overwhelming. Because of their uniqueness, each of them expressed their grief over Loretta's death in different ways.

Val displayed her grief more openly than the others. She cried everyday, especially when she looked at her mother's picture or when someone would mention her mother's death. She withdrew into herself and didn't participate in neighborhood or school activities. She felt guilty, somehow, for her mother's death. She thought that if she had been more helpful around the house, her mother wouldn't have developed a heart problem. Of course, this wasn't logical, but she felt it all the same.

The biggest issue Val had to face, however, was not her guilt, but the intense anger she felt towards her mother for dying, for leaving her behind, and she wasn't even aware that she had this problem to overcome.

Ed expressed his grief over his mother's death in a different way. At first he denied it had even occurred and went off to school the day after the funeral as if nothing had changed. He joked with his friends and even went to the school dance. Ed was told by a friend that time would heal his pain, so he decided that he was going to be tough and would try to keep things as normal as possible. But as time dragged on, the pain inside of him didn't go away and he became very depressed.

About a month after the funeral, Ed began to isolate himself in his room and lost all interest in family activities. He was angry at everyone, but took it out mostly on Val. He would often swear at her for crying over their mother's death. He couldn't understand why she cried so much and she couldn't understand how he could have joked with his friends after the funeral and then attended the school dance.

Charlie wanted to be there for his children, but emotionally he was as bad off as they were. Although he was a mature adult and had read several books about death and dying when his parents died ten years earlier, he wasn't prepared for his wife's untimely death. He felt numb, like a walking, talking zombie going through the motions. He knew his children needed him, but he felt there was nothing inside of him to give.

Charlie's life had been greatly changed by Loretta's death. He was no longer a married man. Now, with less energy than ever before, he had to keep up with his work at the office and the additional domestic duties at home. In some ways he didn't mind the extra work at first because it kept him busy and his mind off his grief. In time, however, he became aware of how lonely he really was. He missed Loretta with all his heart and life no longer seemed fair to him. His dream of a happy family and sharing it all with Loretta was now gone. He became very depressed and there were many nights he cried himself to sleep.

One year after Loretta's death, the family was still having difficulties coping with their grief. It wasn't nearly as bad as it had been during the first few months, but the family was still very unstable. Val often cried at night and was still withdrawn. Ed's grades had gone down and he was constantly getting into trouble at school. Charlie would go into mild depressions for days at a time. The depressions were worse during the holidays, birthdays and special occasions. The Wilsons needed professional help, but Charlie was too overwhelmed by his grief to focus on his family's needs.

Charlie finally decided it was time to do something about the family situation. They couldn't go on living like this, but there wasn't much money in the family budget to cover extra expenses. So he had to make a decision whether to spend what little money they had on professional grief counseling or on a vacation. He called a family meeting to get input from the children. Both Ed and Val wanted to go on a vacation. Ed suggested they borrow a tent and go camping. Val wanted to visit Montreal, because that was where Loretta had always wanted to go. Charlie suggested that counseling would be the best choice, but Ed and Val had no interest in counseling.

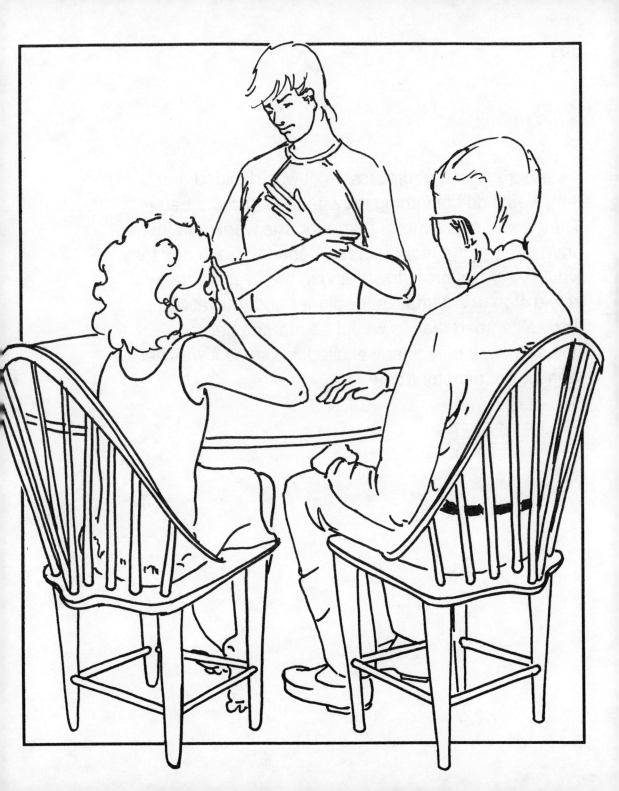

After an hour of discussion, it was decided that they would do something they had never done before. They would rent a motor home for one week and just drive through the mountains of Canada. Each day they would visit a different town, and in the evening they would stop at a campsite for dinner and relaxation. They all agreed the trip would be fun and helpful. Val, however, was particularly excited, because it was her idea to rent a motor home.

About a week later the Wilsons left for Canada. It was their first major trip as a family since Loretta's death. They didn't know exactly where they were going or what they would find, but the anticipation of discovering something new made it all very exciting.

The family was prepared for all types of weather and situations. They had packed bathing suits, summer shorts, rain parkas, long johns and even winter jackets. They had enough camping and fishing equipment to supply an army, and they had enough junk food stuffed in the corners of the motor home to last a month. They were totally prepared for their special outing and they all knew the vacation would be helpful in healing the family, but what they didn't plan for was the miracle that was about to occur on their trip. It would be an event that would change their lives forever.

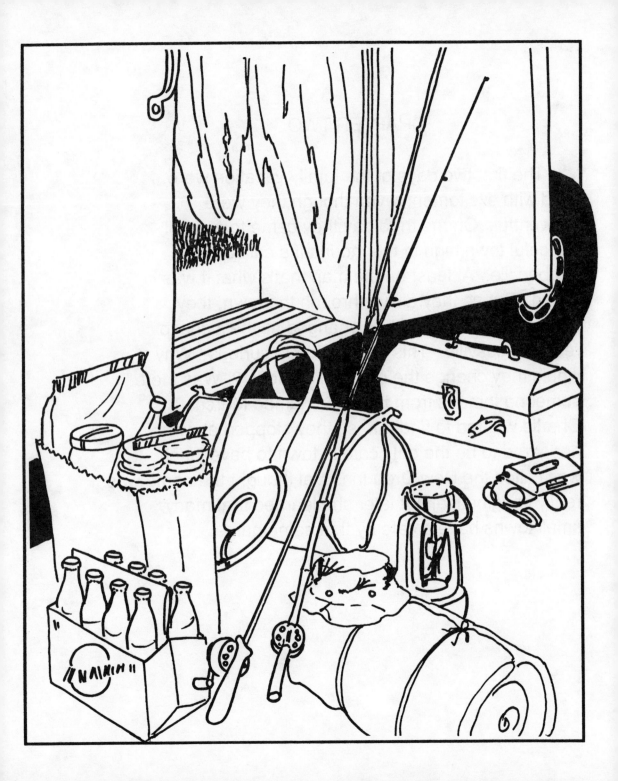

CHAPTER TWO

The first two days of the family vacation were filled with excitement, even though they were uneventful. On the third day they came to a small, peaceful town high in the mountains called Timberville. At least on the map that's what it was called. But as they drove through the town, they noticed that someone had changed all the signs to read Marcusville. This made Charlie curious. Why would they change the name of the town? Was there someone famous from this area named Marcus? Charlie wanted to find out, so they stopped at what appeared to be the only cafe in town to have lunch. It was called the Dew Drop Inn. Val thought the name was really imaginative, but later she learned that many small towns have a cafe by that same name.

As Charlie, Val and Ed entered the cafe, they were surprised to find it filled with so many customers. But the people weren't eating or drinking, they were just sitting at the tables and talking. Talking about a person named Marcus. Talking about the latest miracle he had performed. Talking about how he had revived a young boy who had drowned earlier that morning. Talking about how the town had been so blessed with such a wonderful spiritual teacher.

Val was the first to mention that she wanted to meet Marcus. She thought secretly to herself that, since Marcus could perform miracles, maybe he could bring her mother back to life.

Ed had no interest in meeting him. He was on vacation and the last person he wanted to meet was another teacher. He saw enough teachers during the school year.

But Charlie insisted that they find Marcus and talk to him about Loretta's death. He believed it was the right thing to do and, besides, he had many unanswered questions about death and dying that maybe Marcus could answer. He had also read several books about the near-death experience and wanted a spiritual teacher to explain it to him.

Charlie asked the waitress to draw a map to Marcus' cabin. After lunch they drove out to visit him.

Marcus lived only three miles out of town, but the dirt road to his house was so filled with pot holes that it took about twenty minutes to get there. His home was small and simple. It was a brown wood-frame house on the edge of a crystal-clear lake. The setting was extremely peaceful.

As the Wilsons walked to the back of the house, they noticed a family of squirrels playing in the yard and several swans swimming near the boat dock. Charlie walked out on the dock to see if there were any fish in the water, and as he did, he heard someone yell from the cabin, "Make yourself at home. I'll be there in a minute." Charlie wondered if that was Marcus' voice.

42

Soon a tall, thin man with a dog came walking out
of the house. He wore a sky blue sweater that
matched his eyes and an old pair of jeans that were
splattered with white paint. He was clean shaven and
actually very distinguished looking considering his
casual attire. The dog had a stiff harness around his
body, similar to that of a seeing-eye-dog.

"He's blind," Val whispered to Ed.

"I don't think so," Ed replied, since Marcus was able
to step over all the obstacles in the yard.

With a big smile he held out his hand and said,
"Hello. Welcome to my home. My name is Marcus and
this is my dog, Calib."

Charlie introduced himself and his children and
then apologized for not calling first before coming
out.

Marcus accepted the apology, then laughed and
said, "You couldn't have reached me anyway, since I
don't have a phone."

His warm laughter erased all feelings of
uneasiness.

"I'm going to take my dog for a walk around the lake. Would you like to join me?"

"Sounds great," Charlie enthusiastically replied.

"My dog's getting old and he needs all the exercise he can get."

Val looked at the dog and asked, "How long have you had your seeing-eye-dog?"

Marcus laughed heartily, "Calib isn't a seeing-eye-dog and I'm not blind. Actually, it's the other way around. Calib's blind and this harness keeps him from running into things when we go for walks. I guess you might call me his seeing-eye-man."

Ed and Val petted Calib, then ran off ahead, as Charlie walked with Marcus.

After walking for awhile, Marcus turned to Charlie and looked deep into his eyes. "I sense a great deal of sorrow in your soul. Are you grieving the loss of a loved one?"

Charlie was taken aback by Marcus' perception. How did Marcus know there was anything wrong with him? He hadn't said anything about his deceased wife. He nodded slightly, trying to gather the words to express his feelings.

"How long have you been grieving Loretta's death?"

Charlie was startled at hearing Loretta's name. How could Marcus know anything about Loretta? Charlie's eyes began to water as memories of her flashed through his mind. The tears started to roll down his cheeks. Feeling light-headed, he sat on the sand and then started to sob. Marcus sat down next to him, put his arm around his shoulder and held him as he cried.

Once Charlie had regained his composure, he told
Marcus that his wife, Loretta, had died a year earlier
and that the family was having great difficulty coping
with her loss. "We heard about you in town and
thought that you might be able to help us."

"I'll try to do whatever I can," Marcus replied as he
silently prayed for the words to help the family.

Charlie called for Val and Ed to join them and then
explained that he thought that Marcus could answer all
their questions about their mother's death.

Although both Val and Ed liked Marcus, they really
weren't sure that this man could help them. After all,
he didn't know them or their mother. Val broke the
silence first by asking Marcus, "Is my mother living
with God now?"

Marcus smiled warmly and answered, "Yes, she is
living with God now. But she was also living with God
before she died, just as we all are. You see, God isn't
some distant person, but is a spirit that permeates
the whole universe. A part of this spirit lives within
you, Val, and everyone else."

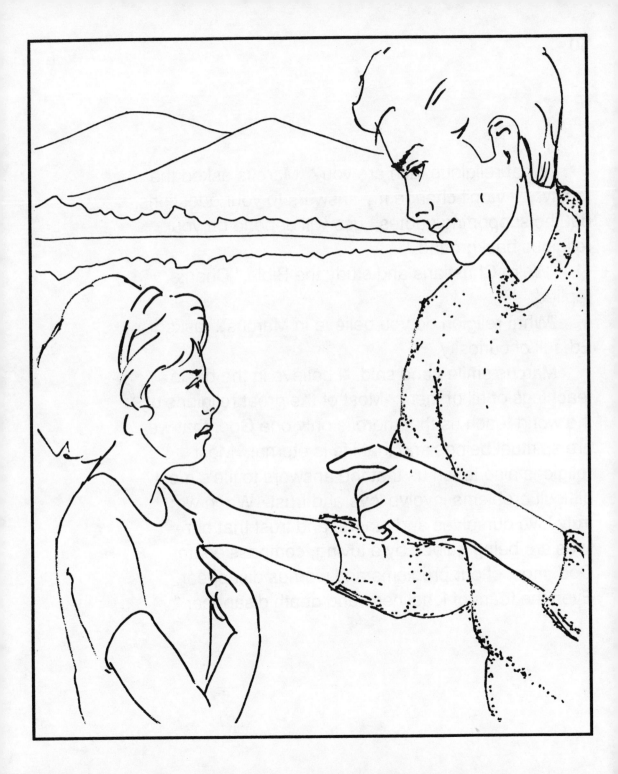

50

"What religious faith are you?" Marcus asked the family. "It won't change my answers to your questions, but the supporting quotes I use will depend on your religious background."

"We're Christians and study the Bible," Charlie replied.

"What religion do you believe in Marcus?" asked Ed, full of curiosity.

Marcus smiled and said, "I believe in the basic teachings of all of them. Most of the great religions of the world teach us that there is only one God, that we are spiritual beings and that life is eternal. Most religions also teach us that the answers to life's most difficult problems involve love and trust. When we truly love ourselves and others, and trust that our lives are being guided by a loving, compassionate God, most of our problems and worries disappear. Even the fears of loneliness and death disappear."

"Are you saying that we wouldn't fear death and loneliness if we had a more thorough understanding of God?" asked Ed.

"Yes, that's precisely what I'm saying," answered Marcus.

"Then tell us, Marcus, who exactly is God?" questioned Ed.

Marcus smiled and said, "I can't tell you exactly who God is, because I don't know that answer. God is much more than our minds can conceive. But there are many passages in the Bible that give us information about God. Some of the most important passages are:

> God is a spirit.
> God is love.
> God is full of compassion.
> There is only one God.
> God is not a man.
> We are all God's children.

Marcus continued, "There is one other verse that you may want to read. It's 1 Corinthians 6:19. Basically, it says the Spirit of God, the Holy Spirit, lives within each of us."

"Are you suggesting that we are more than just human beings?" Charlie inquired.

"Many of us can't believe more than what our five senses tell us and they tell us that we are just human beings with limited powers living in a physical world. But we are much more than that. Our total being consists of two parts. We have both physical and spiritual identities. They are separate identities that occupy the same space. Our physical identity consists of our human body and ego. It's our flesh and blood. This is the part of us that grew from a baby into an adult and will someday die and be buried. This is the part of us that is described in Darwin's Theory of Evolution when he said that man evolved from the lower animal kingdom. This is the part of us the Bible says will 'return to dust' when we die. The main purpose of our physical identity is to provide a vehicle, a means of transportation, for our spiritual identity." Marcus looked at the children to be sure he had their attention.

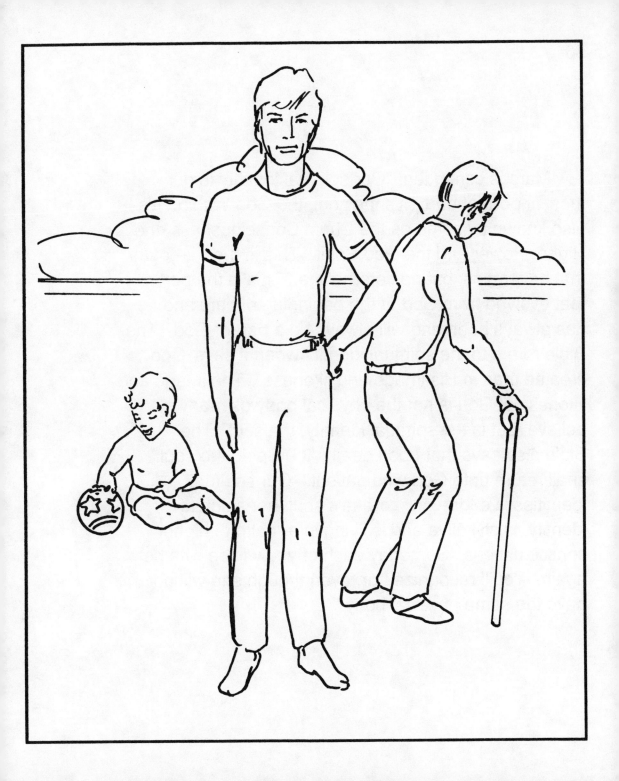

Marcus continued, "Our spiritual identity is our most important part. It's the soul, the God Within. It's also known by some as the Christ Consciousness, the Higher Power and the God Spirit. This is the part of us that never dies, but has eternal life. This is the part that evolved from God at the beginning of time and has always been and will always be a part of God. The Bible refers to the spiritual identity when it says 'God created man in His image and likeness.' The image and likeness of God is not the physical body as many believe, but is the spiritual identity, the soul. The Bible also says that upon death, 'the Spirit, the soul shall return unto God who gave it.' Our spiritual identities live forever. Loretta's soul, her spiritual identity, is still alive and is living in a realm of higher consciousness. Someday each of you will be with her again. You'll recognize her, even though she will not have the same physical body."

"Will she appear to us as a 'being of light' as described in so many books on near-death experiences?" asked Charlie.

"Yes, she will," answered Marcus. "The thousands of near-death experiences that have been reported around the world during the last thirty years have provided mankind with a phenomenal insight into the afterlife. Some skeptics and atheists have tried to discredit the research studies, but have failed to do so. In fact, the near-death experience, or NDE for short, is the best proof we have of the afterlife."

Marcus could tell from Ed and Val's blank expressions that they didn't know what he was talking about. "Do you want me to explain what a near-death experience is and the stages a person goes through at the time of death, the moment their spiritual identity separates from their physical body?"

They nodded for him to tell them more.

"Before you can understand the significance of the near-death experience," Marcus said, "it's important to understand exactly what human death is. Human death is the soul's movement from one plane of consciousness to another. It's a natural step in the evolution of the soul. Although the human body and the negative personality traits of the ego are left behind, the loving qualities of the soul continue to live. Death is a very freeing experience. The soul is no longer restricted by erroneous thoughts and a limited body. An analogy of death would be the movement from a confining, painful situation to a beautiful garden filled with friends, love and peace. Death is actually a rebirth for the soul that is more miraculous than the birth of a human being! It's an experience that was designed by our loving, compassionate God. When death occurs, the soul celebrates its completion of an important task on earth and then moves on."

"Marcus, you make it sound like our souls have a purpose for living on earth. Is that true?" asked Charlie.

"That's exactly right," said Marcus. "Our souls are here to correct minor imperfections that exist within them. These minor imperfections are corrected as we feel and express our emotions as human beings. The situations that we experience on earth are exactly what each of us need to correct the imperfections. After these imperfections are corrected, our souls leave our human bodies and move on to a higher consciousness. Death of the human body doesn't occur until the soul is ready to move on. From a spiritual perspective, there is no such thing as a premature or accidental death. This is a very important, yet difficult, point to understand. The events in this world are controlled by our souls, our spiritual identities. Our souls are infinitely more powerful than our human personalities, our limited egos."

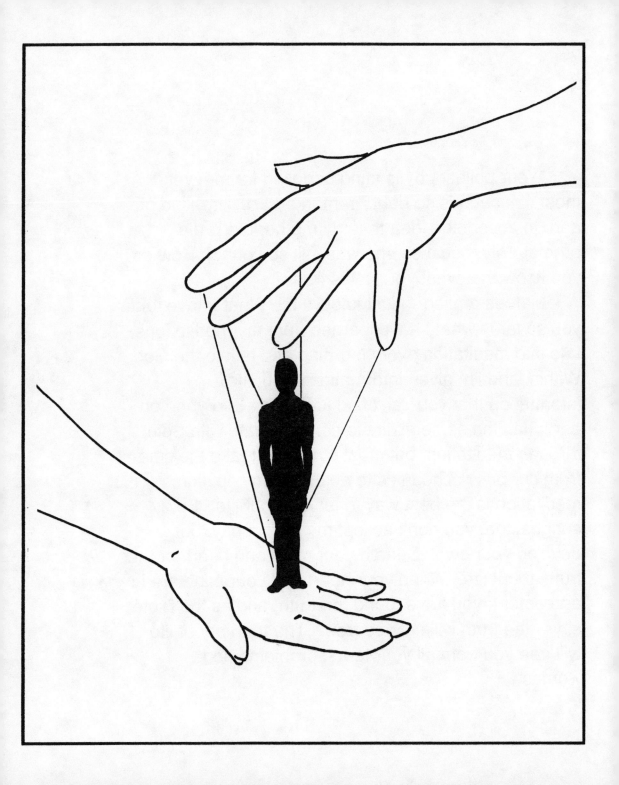

"Your philosophy is mind boggling for me, yet most of it sounds so right," remarked Ed. "It's kind of hard to accept the idea that my mother didn't die prematurely, because she was still so young. How do you know that what you say is true?"

Marcus replied, "I just know it is. What I have told you so far is what I have learned from my meditations. I go into meditation every morning and talk to the God Within, and I'm given information about life, information that you can't find in books. Everyone on earth has the same ability to communicate with Spirit through meditation, but most of us don't take the time from our busy schedules to do so. In my opinion, meditation is the best way to learn about life. Ed, I suggest that you don't accept my philosophy, but develop your own. Search your mind and heart for the truth about life. When your heart and your mind are in agreement, you have found the truth, and as the Bible says, 'the truth will set you free.' The truth about life will free you from all your fears, problems and worries."

66

"I think Calib is getting restless. Why don't we walk for awhile and then I'll answer your questions. There's an ice cream stand not too far from here, if you're interested?"

"Sounds great to me, Marcus!" exclaimed Edward, never one to turn down food.

"After we get our ice cream, I want to hear more about the near-death experience," stated Val. "I want to know why my mother will appear to me someday as a 'being of light.' I also want to know what else my mother is doing in the afterlife."

Marcus smiled at Val and said, "I'll tell you everything you need to know."

CHAPTER THREE

After eating ice cream, Charlie, Ed, Val and Marcus continued their walk on the beach. Calib was at Marcus' side as usual. They didn't get very far before Val said, "Marcus, please explain what a near-death experience is."

"Certainly, Val." Marcus smiled. He was pleased to see her inquisitive nature. "A near-death experience is a very special event that occurs when someone is dying. During a NDE, as it's often called, the human body dies and the spiritual identity, the soul, separates itself from the physical body and goes on to a higher consciousness. While in this higher consciousness the soul experiences one or more stages of the pre-afterlife. During any one of these stages the soul may be directed to return to earth to continue its life. A person who has experienced a clinical death and any of the stages of the pre-afterlife is said to have had a near-death experience. It's now believed that several million people on earth have had this experience, but it's only recently that some are willing to talk about it."

"Marcus, what are the stages of the near-death experience and do only older people have them?" Ed asked.

Marcus smiled at Ed and answered, "If you read some of the latest books on the near-death experience, you'll find that various researchers have categorized the NDE stages differently. But the individual experiences they have analyzed are very similar and most of them fall within well-defined stages. There are seven stages I'll describe to you that encompass the total experience, but first, let me answer your second question. As far as age is concerned, all age groups have had near-death experiences. In fact, they are independent of age, race, religious background and sex. This shouldn't be surprising to you, since everyone on earth is equal from a spiritual perspective, and everyone has spiritual and physical identities. In God's eyes, we are all equal."

Marcus continued, "So let me now describe to you the seven stages of the near-death experience. I have already asked the God Within, the Holy Spirit as some Christians call it, to help me explain to you what happened the moment Loretta died and what her spiritual identity, her soul, is doing now. Sometimes Spirit speaks through me when I don't know exactly what to say. But first, let us pray together that our minds and hearts will be open to the information that we are about to receive."

The four of them stood in a circle, held hands and bowed their heads as Marcus said a short prayer. He prayed, "Dear Heavenly Father, three of your children are grieving the death of a loved one. Please bring comfort to their souls by providing them with the knowledge they seek. Thank you, God. Amen."

They all stood motionless for a few minutes after the prayer knowing that something special was about to happen, then they sat down on the sand and waited.

At first there was only silence. Marcus just looked
at each of them and smiled. Then he got up and
removed the harness from Calib's body. Calib
followed Marcus back to the group and sat down next
to him. He put his head on Marcus' lap and rested as
his sightless eyes stared aimlessly. Marcus lovingly
petted his faithful companion and then asked, "Did
Loretta die in the kitchen of your home last year from
a heart attack?"

Memories of finding Loretta lying on the kitchen
floor flashed through Charlie's mind as he answered in
a quiet voice, "Yes."

Again there were several minutes of silence
before Marcus said, "Are you aware that her last
thoughts were about how beautiful her life was and
how she had been blessed with a wonderful family and
many friends?"

Marcus turned to Ed and said, "On her last day, she
was also wondering if you were going to wear your
black shirt with the red snakes and purple lizards to
the picnic."

Marcus' insight had definitely captured Ed's full attention. How could Marcus know anything about that old black shirt that he wore to the community picnic? Especially since he had thrown it out last winter.

Marcus continued, "As Loretta was dying, her human body experienced some pain from the heart attack, but it was very minimal. A few seconds later she entered the first stage of the near-death experience. Stage One is called the Out-of-Body Experience. During this stage the soul, the spiritual identity, separates itself from the human body, the physical identity. Some people have reported hearing strange sounds when this happens. Other people have reported seeing an illuminated spirit rising up from a dying body. Personally, I have not heard or seen anything like this, but then, there are many people who have supernatural senses that are much sharper than mine."

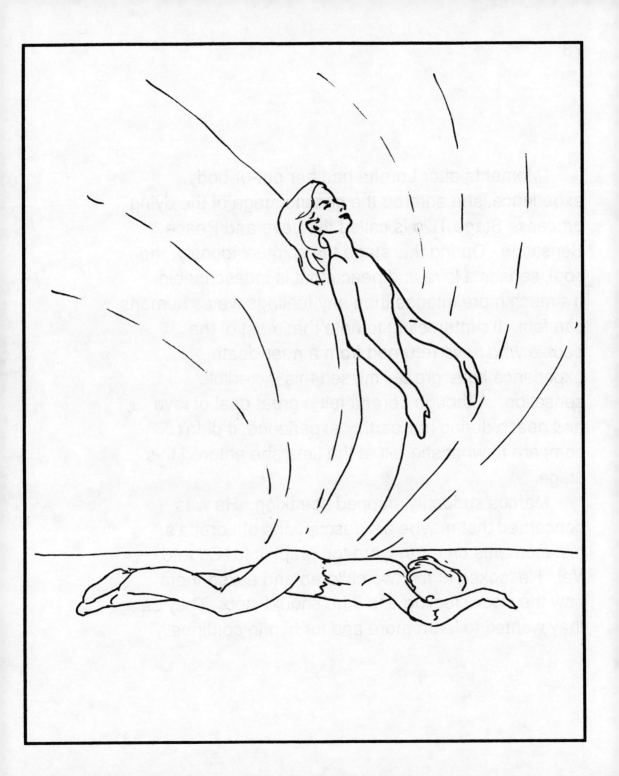

"Moments after Loretta had her out-of-body experience, she entered the second stage of the dying process. Stage Two is called the Love and Peace Sensation. During this stage the spiritual identity, the soul, senses a love and peace that is indescribable. It's much more intense than any feelings we as humans can feel. It's interesting to note that most of the people who have returned from a near-death experience have greatly missed this incredible sensation. Although Loretta felt a great deal of love and peace during her earthly experience, it didn't compare to what she felt at the time she entered this stage."

Marcus suddenly stopped speaking. He was concerned that maybe his descriptions of Loretta's last moments on earth were too graphic for Ed and Val. He looked at the two children and asked them how they were feeling and if he should stop. They said they wanted to learn more and for him to continue.

"I have a question," said Charlie. "Did Loretta know she was dying when she was having the out-of-body experience?"

"She knew within a few seconds what was happening. You see, the first three stages of the dying process all occur within a few seconds of each other. The Third Stage of the dying process is called the Awareness of Death and Surroundings stage. It's in this stage the soul understands it has separated from the physical body and that human death has occurred. It's also in this stage that the soul recognizes the events that surrounded its transition. Shortly after Loretta's soul had separated itself from the physical body, it became aware that she had died of a heart attack in the kitchen. Her soul was also aware that no one else was in the house at the time of her death. While in this stage, her soul visited each of you at the park where you were preparing for the community picnic."

"I don't remember seeing her," said Val. "Did I see her?"

"No, you didn't see her, but you had loving thoughts of her as her soul visited you," replied Marcus. "Her soul was watching over you when you spilt the gallon of pink lemonade all over the white tablecloth."

Val was startled and asked, "How did you know about that? I didn't tell anyone that I was the one who did it!"

Marcus just smiled, looked at Ed and Charlie, and continued with his story. "Her soul was also with the two of you when you were deciding which type of flowers to give her when she received her award. Do you remember your conversation about the flowers?"

Charlie replied, "Yes, we decided to give her four red roses, one for each member of the family. She loved roses."

"Will her soul ever visit us again?" asked Ed.

"Yes, her soul will visit you again. In fact, it has visited each one of you many times since her death."

"After visiting the three of you in the park, Loretta's soul entered Stage Four of the dying process. This stage is called the Journey to Higher Consciousness. In this stage her soul, encapsulated in an invisible shell of incredible love and peace, floated effortlessly through a dimly lit tunnel towards a bright light. There was never any fear of what was happening. And by the time she reached the end of the tunnel, she was aware that everything in the universe had a purpose and that everyone was totally protected by a loving Spirit."

Val asked, "Wasn't she worried about us? What about all the heartaches and problems her death would cause us? It doesn't seem like her to just leave us like that."

Marcus replied gently, "By the time she completed stage four, she understood there was a reason for her death and that only opportunities, not insurmountable problems, would result from it. Her death provided opportunities for all those she touched to grow spiritually."

"Loretta really enjoyed the fifth stage of her death experience," said Marcus. "Most spirits do. It's like going to a party and seeing many old friends. This stage is actually called the Greeting by Friends."

Charlie interrupted and said, "I have read about this stage, Marcus. Isn't this where your deceased parents and relatives meet you?"

"Yes, but many other souls also meet you at this stage, not just relatives."

Ed enthusiastically asked, "Do you know who was there to meet her? How did they look? Were there many spirits? Were my grandparents there?"

Marcus laughed and said, "I can answer all your questions, Ed, but let's take them one at a time. When your mother entered this stage of the dying process, she was greeted by eleven beings of light. Each of these beings of light was a soul that had played a major part in her own soul development. She had known most of these souls for a very long time."

"Who was there, Marcus? Can you give us their names?" Charlie asked patiently.

"I will tell you who the eleven spirits were, but you won't recognize some of them," answered Marcus. "Some of them were souls who greatly helped her many years before you knew her. The first souls she met were Ray and Mildred Kingsley. Do you remember who they were?"

Charlie replied, "Sure, they were her parents. Both of them died when Loretta was a teenager."

"The third soul she met was Don Kingsley," said Marcus.

"That was Loretta's youngest brother. He was killed in an accident about five years ago in Cleveland," remarked Charlie. "Don was crossing a street and was hit by a car that was driven by an intoxicated politician. The man wasn't held responsible for the accident and was set free. Just last year I read that the politician died in a plane accident. Loretta's brother was a wonderful man and I know she missed him a great deal."

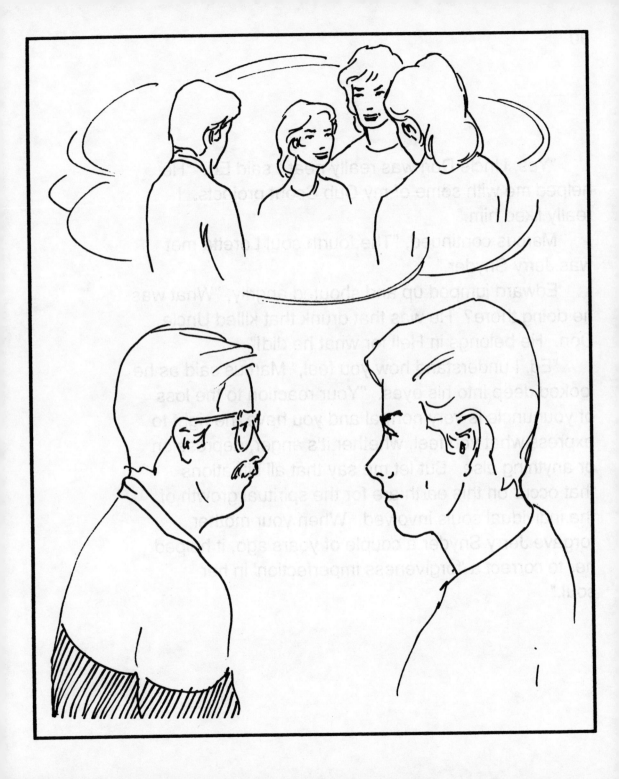

"Yes, Uncle Don was really neat," said Ed. "He helped me with some of my Cub Scout projects. I really liked him."

Marcus continued, "The fourth soul Loretta met was Jerry Snyder."

Edward jumped up and shouted angrily, "What was he doing there? He was that drunk that killed Uncle Don. He belongs in Hell for what he did!"

"Ed, I understand how you feel," Marcus said as he looked deep into his eyes. "Your reaction to the loss of your uncle is very normal and you have the right to express what you feel, whether it's anger, depression or anything else. But let me say that all situations that occur on this earth are for the spiritual growth of the individual souls involved. When your mother forgave Jerry Snyder a couple of years ago, it helped her to correct a 'forgiveness imperfection' in her soul."

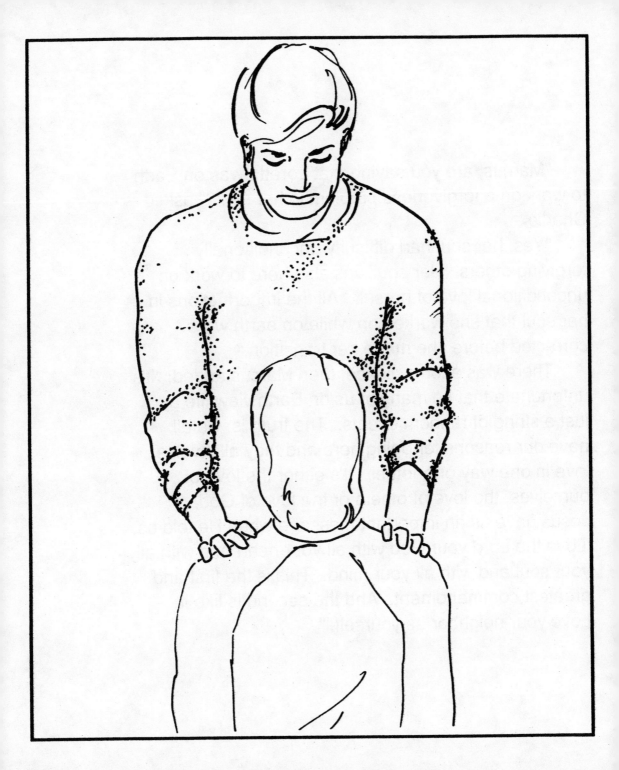

"Marcus, are you saying that Loretta was on Earth to work on a forgiveness problem in her soul?" asked Charlie.

"Yes, her soul had difficulty unconditionally forgiving others. Her soul was also here to work on unconditional love of herself. All the imperfections in her soul that she worked on while on earth were corrected before she made her transition."

There was a long silence, then Marcus added, "It's unfortunate that so many of us on Earth view life as just a string of random events. The truth is, we all have our reasons for being here and they all involve love in one way or another. It's either the love of ourselves, the love of others or the love of God. Jesus gave us an important message when He told us, 'Love the Lord your God with all your heart and with all your soul and with all your mind. This is the first and greatest commandment. And the second is like it: Love your neighbor as yourself.'"

There was another long silence as each of them contemplated what Marcus had just said. They were aware that they were good, decent people, but they weren't sure their love for others was unconditional.

Marcus interrupted their thoughts by saying he would give them the names of other beings of light who greeted Loretta. He used his fingers as he counted off the names. "The fifth being of light was her uncle, Tom Cutler; the sixth was a great aunt, Ruth Harper; the seventh was a high school teacher, Abby Carson; the eighth was a spiritual teacher, Mohammed Immaga; the ninth was a spiritual guide, Raphael; the tenth was another spiritual guide, Rhee Tao Pu; and the eleventh was a famous guru named Mocada Ruka."

Marcus looked up from the hand he was counting on and saw confused, blank looks on the faces of his new friends.

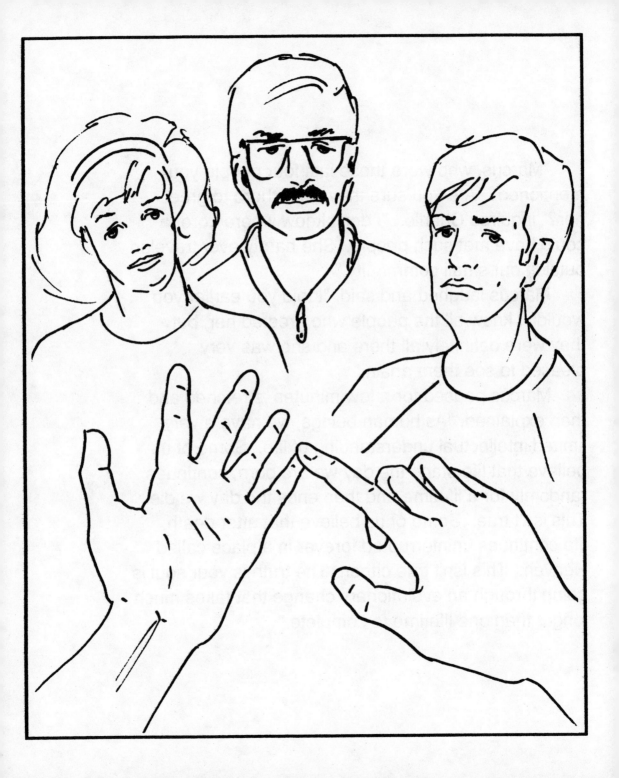

"Marcus, who were those last four people you mentioned? Are you sure they were there to greet her?" inquired Charlie. "I don't know where Loretta could have met such people. She hardly ever traveled outside our small community."

Marcus laughed and said, "I told you earlier you wouldn't know all the people who greeted her, but they were definitely all there and she was very pleased to see them again."

Marcus paused for a few minutes, stretched and then explained, "As human beings, we have a very limited intellectual understanding of life. Some of us believe that life starts the day we are born, continues randomly for a lifetime and then ends the day we die. This isn't true. Some of us believe that after death, life continues uninterrupted forever in a place called Heaven. This isn't true either. The truth is your soul is going through an evolutionary change that takes much longer than one lifetime to complete."

"Are you suggesting that in another lifetime Loretta knew that guru and those spiritual guides who greeted her?" asked Charlie. "That sounds too unbelievable to me."

Marcus nodded, "I know it sounds unbelievable to you, but it's true. Do you realize, Charlie, that if you were born into an Eastern religion such as Hinduism or Buddhism, you would readily accept the concept of reincarnation as being true? You wouldn't even think twice about it. Your disbelief in what I have just told you is only because it doesn't agree with your religious background. Although reincarnation, the rebirth of a soul in another body, is not part of the Christian doctrine, Jesus did talk about it in the Bible when He told his disciples that Elijah had returned as John the Baptist. Elijah had died several hundred years before John was born. Elijah and John the Baptist shared the same soul. Charlie, it's important that you search your heart for the real truth about reincarnation. It's easier to understand and accept death when one believes in it."

Val was fascinated with the beings of light and asked Marcus, "Were there any other beings of light at the party?"

"Yes. After being greeted by her old soul friends, your mother's soul met one of the supreme beings of light. At this time she was entering Stage Six of the dying process, which is called the Greeting by a Supreme Being. All the supreme beings are highly enlightened souls who have lived on the Earth at one time or another during the past few thousand years. Most of these enlightened souls have lived very humble lives while on Earth. Some, however, have held high positions within the organized religions. Only a few of them have been recognized for their spiritual wisdom."

Ed asked, "Jesus is a supreme being, right?"

Marcus replied, "Yes, Jesus is one of them. Some others are Mohammed, Buddha, Confucius and Lao Tse. Each of these supreme beings founded their own great religion while living on Earth."

102

"Who was the supreme being of light who met my mother?" asked Ed. "I bet it was Jesus, since she was a devoted Christian."

Marcus smiled, shook his head and said, "If I were a betting man, I would take you up on that bet, Ed, but I'm not a betting man. The supreme being who met your mother was Gosuda, a Buddhist monk who lived in the mountains of what we now call India. He was last living on this earth about a hundred years before Jesus came. His soul, like the souls of all the other supreme beings of light, overflows with love. Your mother knew of him and felt honored by his visit."

"Aren't there any other Christian supreme beings in the afterlife that could have met my mother?" asked Ed. "Wouldn't she have felt more comfortable with a Christian than with a Buddhist, particularly a Buddhist monk?"

Marcus replied earnestly, "In the afterlife, Ed, there are no separate religions, races or sexes. There is just a 'oneness.' The energy of all the individual souls living within our abundantly alive universe blend together to form a 'oneness' that is so magnificent, so awesome, so glorious that our minds can't comprehend it. This 'oneness' is God. I wish I could explain it to you better, but there are no words in the human language to describe it. If you learn how to deeply meditate, you will get in touch with this energy and you will never worry about anything again."

Marcus stood up, walked to the edge of the water, skipped a few stones across the flat, reflective surface and then returned. Charlie, Ed and Val were still thinking about what Marcus had just said. Marcus stroked Calib's graying coat and then sat down on the sand. He said he wanted to tell them about the last two stages of Loretta's adventure before they finished their walk.

"Stage Seven of the dying process is called the Review of Life," said Marcus. "Loretta's review was conducted by Gosuda, the supreme being who greeted her. During her review, the significant events in her life were flashed in front of her on what appeared to be a three-dimensional panoramic screen. As she sensed the individual events, she felt the emotions of all the souls involved. In the events where she caused pain, she felt the sorrow, and where she brought happiness, she felt the joy. During the review, Loretta also became totally aware of the spiritual purpose of her visit to earth. She learned that she was working on the unconditional forgiveness of others and the unconditional love of herself. At the end of the review, Gosuda asked her if there was any reason she needed to return to earth. Knowing that her family was being protected by a loving Spirit and her spiritual assignment had been completed, she declined the offer to return."

"Marcus, I have read that some souls return to earth after the Review of Life. Is this true?" asked Charlie.

"Yes, it's true. Some souls do return to their human bodies and continue living on earth, but most don't. Most souls at this stage continue on to the final stage of dying, an activity sometimes referred to as R & R. Those souls who do return, do so for one of two reasons. It's either because they want to complete an unfinished spiritual assignment on earth or because they have been told to return by a supreme being. When the supreme being makes the final decision, the soul is often resistant, but still returns."

Marcus looked at Val and saw tears in her eyes. He knew she was feeling rejected because her mother had decided to stay instead of returning home to them. Marcus didn't say anything. He just stretched out his arms for her. She came, they embraced and, as they did, she cried.

Val felt comfortable in Marcus' arms. It gave her a warm, secure feeling of being loved and protected. It was a feeling she hadn't felt since her mother died.

As he held her, Marcus said, "The final stage of the dying process is called the R & R Experience. You may think the letters stand for rest and relaxation, but they don't. The soul, like everything else in God's universe, never reaches a state of idleness. The soul stays active and continues to grow by experiencing new situations. This shouldn't surprise you. Everything that is alive on our planet is changing and growing, so why would it be any different for our living souls? We are told in the Bible that the soul lives forever. This is a true statement, but it doesn't mean that the life of the eternal soul is passive or slumberous. The truth is, the whole universe is abundantly alive and constantly changing, and the same is true for our souls. A loving God designed it that way."

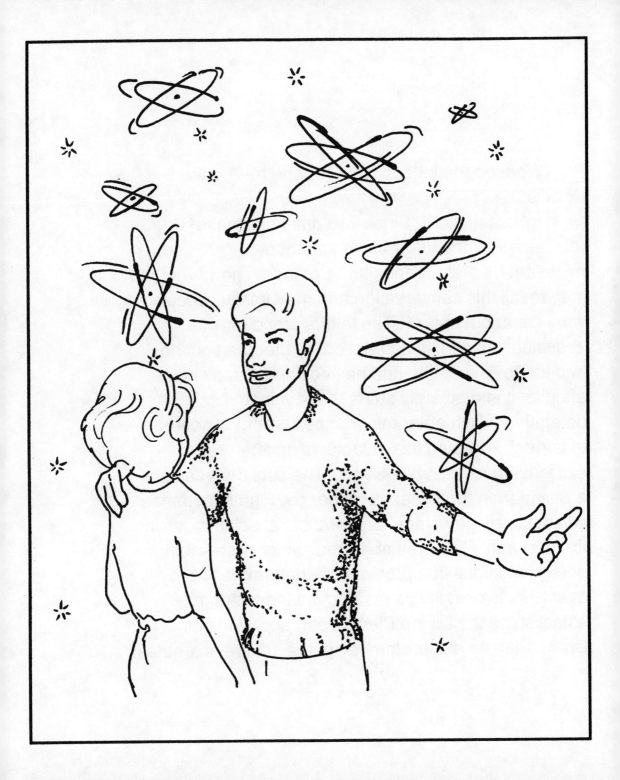

"What do the letters 'R & R' stand for?" asked Charlie.

Marcus replied, "Since you don't believe in reincarnation, the information I'm about to give you might not be that meaningful. Someday, however, you may recall this conversation and may totally accept what I'm about to say. The letters stand for 'reevaluation' and 'reincarnation.' After the soul has had its Review of Life and has decided to stay in the afterlife, it immediately starts to reevaluate itself to determine which other minor imperfections it needs to correct. In doing this, it looks at its total existence over many lifetimes. The soul then designs a Divine Plan for its next experience. The experience can occur on any planet or plane of consciousness in the universe. The Law of Karma, which states that a person's actions in a previous life determine the events in its next life, is the dominating factor in establishing the Divine Plan. Upon approval of the Divine Plan by a supreme being, the soul reincarnates."

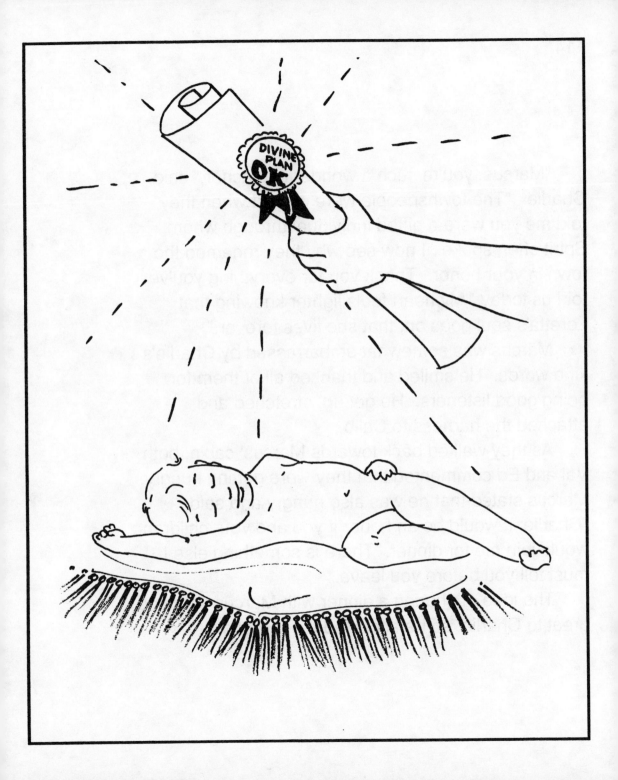

"Marcus, you're such a wonderful teacher," said Charlie. "The townspeople were correct when they told me you were a gifted individual through whom Spirit often spoke. I now see why they renamed the town in your honor. Thank you for everything you've told us today. My heart feels lighter knowing that Loretta's soul goes on, that she lives forever."

Marcus was somewhat embarrassed by Charlie's kind words. He smiled and thanked all of them for being good listeners. He got up, stretched and attached the harness to Calib.

As they walked back towards Marcus' cabin, both Val and Ed commented that they were getting hungry. Marcus stated that he was also hungry and said, "Charlie, it would be an honor if you and your children would join me for dinner. There is something else I must tell you before you leave."

The idea of sharing a dinner with Marcus sounded great to Charlie, so he accepted the invitation.

CHAPTER FOUR

Although Ed and Val enjoyed being with Marcus, the thought of eating dinner with him at his cabin didn't thrill them. Because he was so spiritual, they assumed he probably was some type of vegetarian who only ate certain vegetables, nuts and grains. Ed and Val weren't looking forward to dinner, even though they were quite hungry. They wished their father had declined Marcus' invitation for dinner. They would have preferred to go into town for burgers and fries.

As they waited for dinner, Charlie, who was in the cabin helping Marcus prepare the meal, yelled out to them that dinner would be ready in a few minutes. Five minutes later, Charlie walked into the backyard carrying a tray of food. To the delight of Val and Ed, the tray was filled with hamburgers, fresh corn on the cob, and a tossed salad with tomatoes and cucumbers. As Val and Ed gazed at the food, their thoughts about eating in town vanished.

A few minutes later, Marcus came out of the cabin with a pitcher of lemonade and a box of soft chocolate chip cookies. He was pleased to see that the children were happy with their simple meals. Marcus sat down at the table, said a short prayer and then passed the hamburgers to Val. Noticing that Ed had a grin on his face, Marcus asked him what he was thinking about.

"I was ready to bet Val that we would be eating nuts and vegetables for dinner. I assumed that you were a vegetarian and didn't have any meat in the cabin. But you're not a vegetarian, are you Marcus?"

Marcus smiled and answered, "No, I'm not. Doctors tell us that 'we are what we eat,' and there is definitely some truth to that statement. But a truer statement is 'we are what we believe we are.' The power of belief, in my opinion, overrides the unhealthy effects of the foods we eat. Therefore, I eat all types of foods, but always in moderation."

As the meal was ending, Ed asked Marcus if he had ever been married and if he had any children.

Marcus replied honestly, "I was married once to a wonderful lady for eight years and we had a beautiful daughter named Donna. Donna was killed in a car accident when she was only five years old. I was driving her home from school one day while intoxicated and I crashed the car into a tree. She was the only fatality. Donna's death filled our home with a tremendous amount of grief. There was more grief than my wife and I could handle. As a result, our marriage failed and we divorced."

"I've read that many couples separate or divorce when a child dies. Is that true?" asked Charlie.

"That's true, but it doesn't have to be that way. If people would just take the time to learn about the grieving process, and also accept the fact that each member of their family will cope with the loss in their own unique way, many painful family situations would heal sooner and many family conflicts would be avoided."

Val had a puzzled look on her face. "What exactly is grief? I have heard people say that I'm still grieving Mother's death, but I'm not sure what they mean by that."

Charlie looked at his daughter and said, "From what I've read, grief is an intense emotional suffering caused from a loss. Apparently, the loss can be anything. In fact, the loss doesn't even have to be real, just a perception of a loss will cause the suffering."

"Can you give me some examples, Dad?" asked Val.

"Sure. Some examples would be the loss of a loved one when death occurs, the loss of a spouse during a separation or divorce, the loss of a career at retirement, the loss of a job when fired, the loss of a child who's going off to college and the loss of a friend who's moving away."

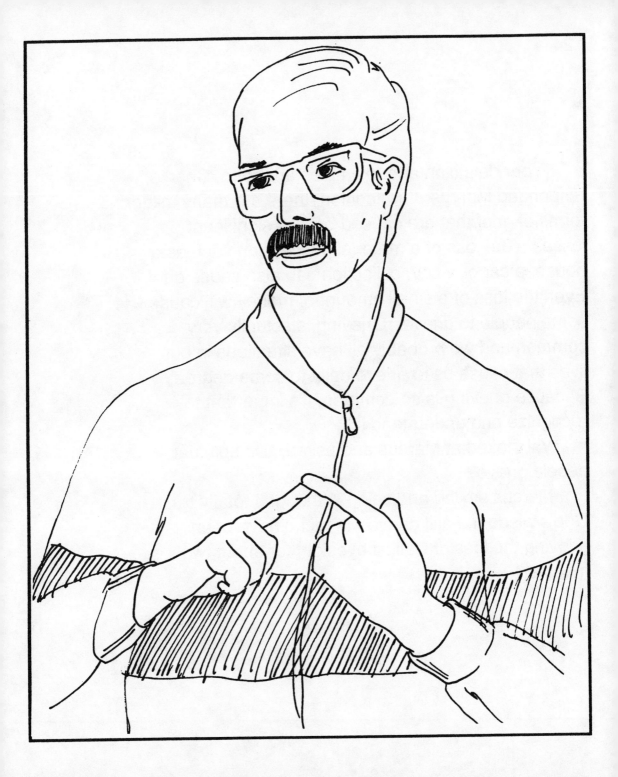

"Your definition and examples are good, Charlie," responded Marcus. "In addition, there are many milder forms of grief that are caused by less significant losses. The loss of a material possession such as a house, a car or a coin collection can also cause grief. Even the loss of a small amount of money will cause some people to grieve. Grieving is actually very common and we probably all have situations in our lives that cause us to grieve daily to some degree. Because grieving is so common, it's important to recognize and understand it."

Val looked at Marcus and asked, "Do spiritual people grieve?"

Marcus smiled and said, "Although I totally trust God's wisdom, I still grieve. In fact, I have been grieving the loss of Calib's eyesight for about two months."

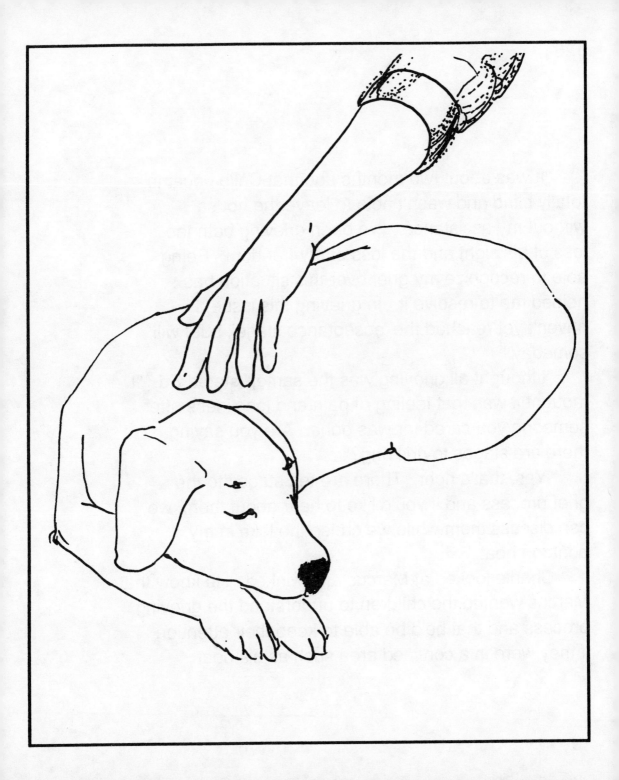

"It was about two months ago that Calib became totally blind and wasn't able to leave the house without my assistance. I've been grieving both the loss of his sight and the loss of my freedom. Being able to recognize my grief over this situation has helped me to resolve it. In grieving this issue, I haven't yet reached the 'acceptance stage', but I will someday."

"I thought all grieving was the same," stated Ed. "I thought it was that feeling of pain and loneliness after someone you cared for was gone. Are you saying there are stages to grieving?"

"Yes, that's right. There are ten stages to the grief process and if you'd like to hear about them, we can discuss them while we cruise the lake in my pontoon boat."

Charlie looked at Marcus and winked. He knew that Marcus wanted the children to understand the grieving process and that he'd be able to keep their attention if they were in a confined area such as his boat.

After dinner was over, Ed grabbed a handful of chocolate chip cookies and strolled down to the dock with Marcus. He wanted to help him prepare the pontoon boat for the evening cruise. Marcus removed the protective boat cover, checked to see if the life jackets were aboard and made sure there was plenty of gas. Everything seemed to be fine and, within minutes, they were cruising the lake.

It was a beautiful evening and the air was calm and cool. The reflective surface of the water mirrored the pine covered mountains and the multicolored sky. The images on the lake were disturbed only by the surfacing of the feeding fish and the ripples from the gliding swans. The scene was an artist's delight.

Val looked at Marcus and said, "I feel so good right now. Is this how I'll feel in Heaven?"

"You'll feel even better. We aren't capable of experiencing on earth the feelings we'll have in the afterlife."

After cruising for about ten minutes, Marcus stopped the engine. "Ed, you asked me about the grieving stages, so let me tell you a few things about them. It may take me awhile, but I think it will help you if I explain what I went through when I was grieving the loss of my wife and daughter."

Val and Ed agreed to listen. They were curious to learn more about what Marcus had been through and whether or not it could help them understand their own grief.

Marcus started his explanation by stating the ten stages of the grieving process. The stages that Marcus listed were:

- Denial
- Isolation
- Anger
- Guilt
- Shame
- Bargaining
- Depression
- Understanding
- Acceptance
- Forgiveness

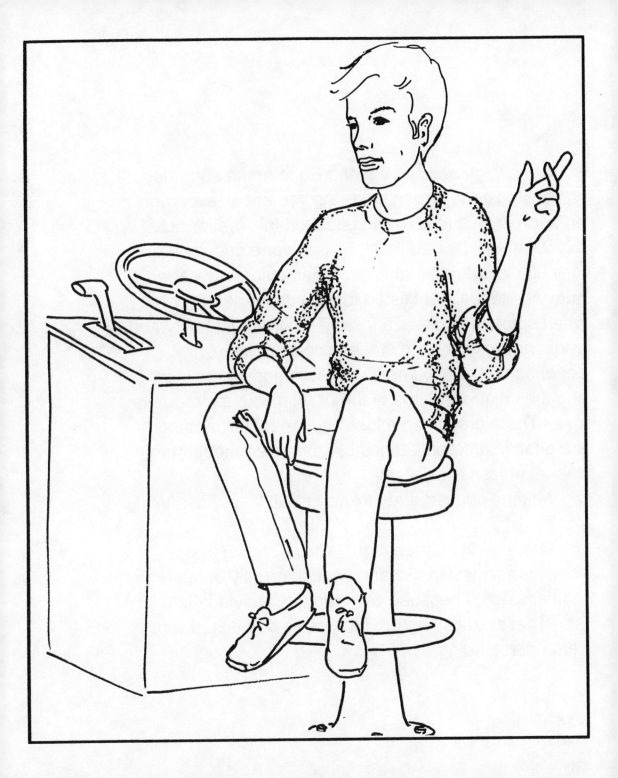

Marcus glanced at Val and Ed to make sure they were listening and then said, "As you know, everyone on earth is unique. No two people think, feel or act exactly alike. Because of this, everyone grieves the loss of a loved one in their own particular way. The grieving stages that I listed for you occur naturally when someone suffers a loss. The order, intensity and frequency in which the stages occur, however, depends on the circumstances surrounding the loss and the unique feelings of the person who suffered the loss. Therefore, when a loss occurs, family members are often in different stages of grief, even though the degree of loss is the same."

Marcus paused and looked at Val. "Am I confusing you?"

"No, I think I understand. You're saying that sometimes my Dad, Ed and I act differently about my mother's death because we're unique individuals."

"That's exactly right," Marcus said, pleased with her understanding.

"Val, do you remember if you and Ed acted differently during the first couple of weeks following your mother's funeral?" questioned Marcus.

"Yes, we acted differently all right. I felt guilty because I thought my laziness had caused my mother's heart attack. I cried for hours every night because I felt so lonely and full of guilt. I couldn't understand how Ed could act like nothing changed in our lives. He would joke with his friends on the phone and he even went to the school dance the week after her funeral. He acted as if Mother hadn't died and I couldn't stand to be around him. I was so angry at him."

Marcus nodded his head and replied, "Can you see that the two of you were in different stages of the grieving process? Val, you were in the stage called 'guilt' and, Ed, you were in the stage called 'denial.' It's very normal to be in one or the other of these grief stages immediately following a loss."

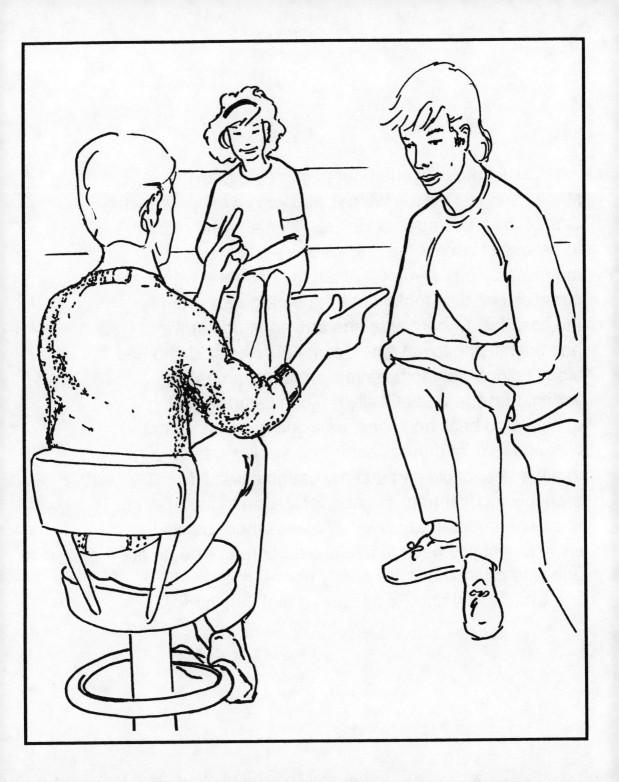

"So, let me tell you about each of the grieving stages and you tell me which ones you've experienced. One of the first stages is 'denial.' Denial is the refusal to believe or accept that the loss has occurred. Let me give you an example. When my daughter was in the car accident, they took her to the emergency room at the hospital. Shortly after she arrived, a doctor, who had been trying to save her, came out and said she had died. I didn't want to believe it and told him he was wrong, that she was still alive. Then I started yelling at him to go back and continue working on her. That was one form of denial. Later that week, I was talking to a friend and told him that my daughter would probably recover from the accident, even though I knew she had already died. That was more denial. Have any of you been in denial over Loretta's death at one time or another? It's a very normal reaction."

Charlie, Val and Ed all agreed that they had.

"Another early stage of grief is called 'isolation,'" stated Marcus. "In this stage people try to isolate or separate themselves both from the loss and from other people who may want to discuss it. Quite often, the stages of isolation and denial overlap. Sometimes people will stay in their houses for days at a time just to avoid others."

Ed said he recognized the stage and added, "There were many days I locked myself in my bedroom and watched hours of television just to avoid talking to Dad and Val about my mother. I just didn't want to see anyone."

"Some people were saying that I was becoming a workaholic after Loretta's death," claimed Charlie. "Is working extra hours on the job part of the isolation stage?"

"It can be," remarked Marcus. "Many people take on extra responsibilities at work to avoid dealing with the loss. Some people bury themselves in their hobbies to keep their minds off their pain. It's not wrong to do this, but it must be done in moderation."

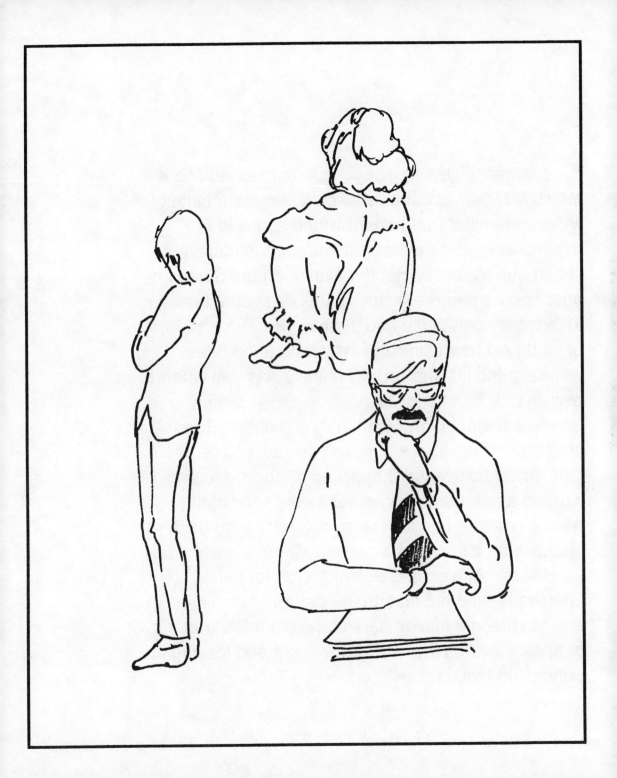

"'Anger' is also an early stage of grieving and it may last for several months," said Marcus. "I think we're all familiar with anger. When a loss is experienced, it's very normal and natural to have it. Unfortunately, our society frowns upon the display of anger and, therefore, many of us just keep it inside. This is very unhealthy and if the anger isn't vented, physical and mental problems will develop."

Val asked, "Who are we usually angry at when a person dies?"

"We are often angry at several people. Sometimes it's the person who we believe has caused the death. Often it's ourselves for not giving enough love and support to the person before they died. Sometimes people even feel angry at the loved one who died, because their leaving has caused them a great deal of loneliness. And occasionally it's God for not intervening and preventing the death."

Val thought for awhile and said, "I think I have a lot of anger towards my mother for dying and leaving me behind. In fact, I know I do."

Charlie put his arm around his daughter and held her as Marcus continued. "Another stage of grieving is called 'guilt.' Guilt is a painful feeling of having done something wrong. It results from one's personal perspective and has nothing to do with society's laws. In dealing with guilt, it's important to remember that, from a spiritual viewpoint, humans do not cause the deaths of other humans. The final decision for human death is always made by the soul of the person who is about to die. As humans, we are only involved in the death, never the cause of death. This is difficult to understand, but it's true."

Marcus paused for awhile, took Val's hand and said, "Val, it's important you understand that the fact that you didn't help your mother more with the housework had nothing to do with her death. Her soul had already decided to leave her human body on that day and nothing you could have done would have prevented it."

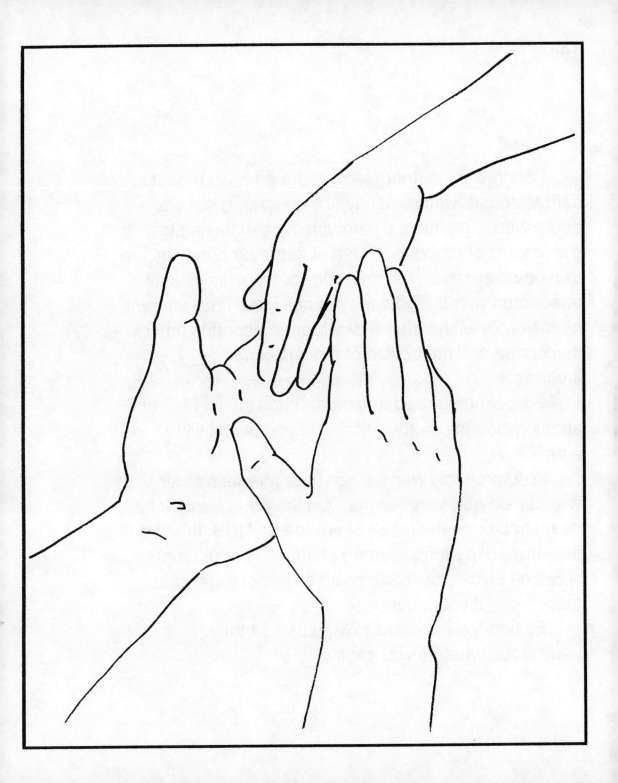

"'Shame' is another stage of the grieving process," said Marcus. "Unfortunately, it's one that is not often addressed. Shame is a painful feeling of having lost the respect of others because of improper behavior. In a death situation, the improper behavior is usually associated with the person who has died. The amount of shame resulting from a death often depends on how it occurred and the beliefs of the individuals involved."

Ed looked puzzled and said, "I don't think I felt any shame when my mother died. Do you think I will later?"

"You probably won't, since your mother's death was considered very natural. On the other hand, if her death had been the result of suicide or AIDS, then you may have experienced some shame. Your personal views on suicide or AIDS would have determined the magnitude of your shame."

Ed and Val indicated to Marcus that they understood what he was saying.

"Another stage of the grieving process is called 'bargaining,'" stated Marcus. "It's a very short lived stage, but it usually happens. During bargaining, a person tries to reverse the events that caused the loss by making an agreement with a higher authority. As an example, when my daughter, Donna, was dying in the hospital after the car accident, I was trying to make deals with both the doctor and with God. I remember telling the doctor that if he saved my daughter, I would donate a large sum of money to the hospital. I also remember saying to God that if He allowed my daughter to live, I'd quit drinking, go to A.A. meetings and start attending church again. Bargaining is a real stage of grieving that many of us go through, but it doesn't seem to do much good."

Charlie added, "I also tried to bargain with God when I found my wife dead on the kitchen floor. I told God I would do anything He wanted me to, if He would just bring Loretta back to me, but He didn't."

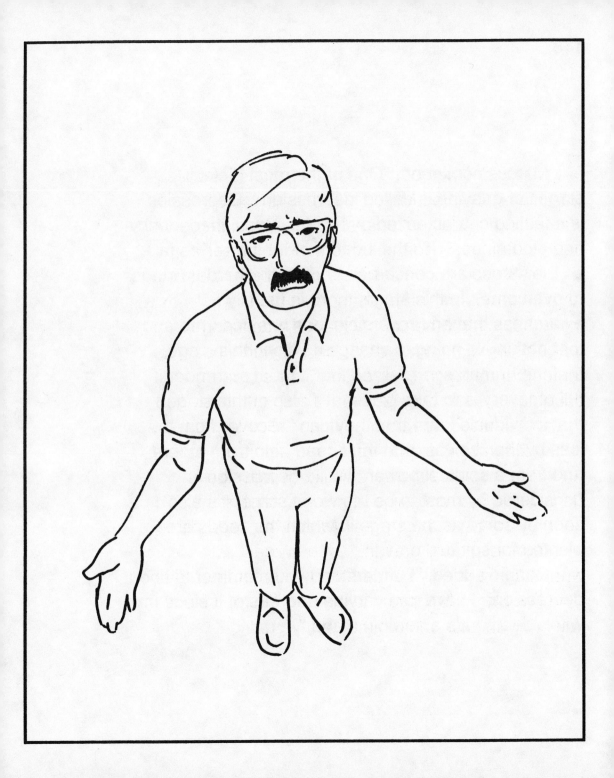

148

Marcus continued, "One of the most difficult stages of grieving is called 'depression.' Depression is a feeling characterized by helplessness, inadequacy and gloominess. It's the 'bottom of the barrel' as far as the stages are concerned and it's the hardest stage to overcome. In this stage, there is usually full awareness that an irreversible loss has occurred and that nothing is going to change it. It's in this stage that the human ego realizes that it must surrender if full recovery is to take place. It's also in this stage that individuals learn that they can't recover from the loss by themselves, that they need help from others and from a spiritual power. While depression is considered by most to be the worst stage, it's also seen by some as the stage in which the seeds are planted for spiritual growth."

Charlie added, "I understand your comments about depression. I have had varying degrees of it since my wife's death. It's a horrible stage."

"'Understanding' is one of the last stages of the grieving process," continued Marcus. "In this stage, there is a comprehension of the facts regarding the loss. This comprehension can occur either as an intellectual understanding, as an intuitive feeling or as both. It all depends on the nature of the person involved."

"Where does information about death come from?" questioned Ed.

"It can come from many sources such as support groups, self-help books and church sermons."

Charlie asked, "What is the best thing we can do to understand our feelings and the circumstances pertaining to Loretta's death?"

Marcus smiled and said, "Attend a 'grief and loss' support group. Every community has some. Often they are held weekly in churches, hospitals, schools, funeral homes or community centers. The open, frank discussions are extremely important."

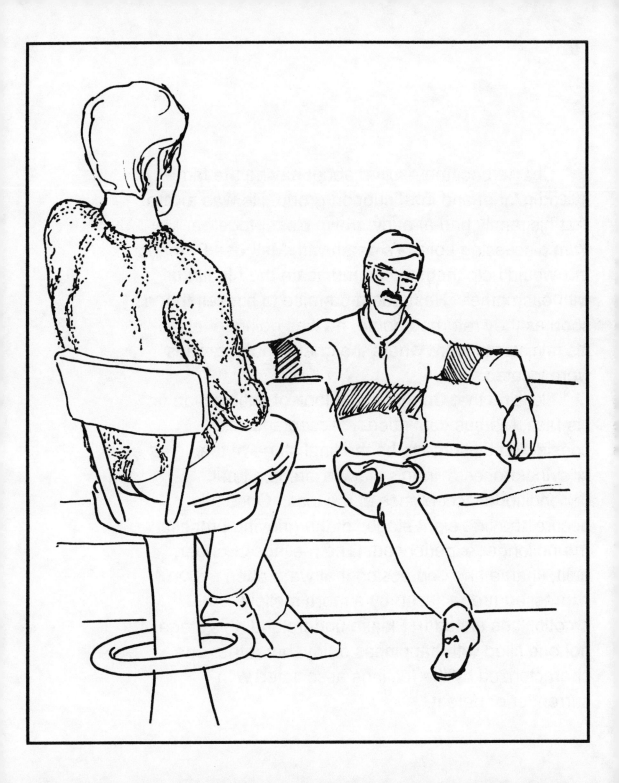

Charlie became excited about having the family attend a 'grief and loss' support group. He was aware that his family had already grown closer together just from discussing Loretta's death with Marcus. Perhaps this would help them to communicate their feelings with each other. He made a promise to himself that as soon as they returned home, he was going to talk to his minister to learn where the grief support groups were located.

Noticing that Charlie had a look of satisfaction on his face, Marcus continued. "'Acceptance' is considered by some to be the final stage of the grieving process. In this stage there is a total, unconditional acceptance of the loss. Once this occurs, the first eight stages of the grieving process are no longer experienced. The feelings of anger, guilt, shame and depression that were often expressed are replaced by a more mellow, emotionless attitude. Please understand, this stage is not one filled with happiness or joy, but rather one characterized by the feelings associated with surrender or defeat."

Marcus continued, "In my opinion, the final stage of the grieving process is not 'acceptance' as some teach, but 'forgiveness.' The forgiveness stage without a doubt is the most important one from a spiritual perspective. It's an activity that some grief counselors don't recognize as a grieving stage, but I believe it's a necessary step to bring closure to an earthly relationship. During the forgiveness stage, a person who has already accepted the loss, gives up all resentment towards those involved in it. In this stage, all desires to punish others disappear. As humans, we have difficulty forgiving others, but until this last stage is completed, total healing of the loss does not occur. It should be noted that forgiveness is done to bring freedom and peace of mind to the forgiver, not to the one being forgiven. It's the forgiver who benefits from the forgiveness process."

Marcus added, "When my daughter died in the car accident, I had several people to forgive, most of all, myself. My emotional freedom from this loss didn't occur until unconditional forgiveness of all those involved had taken place. Once this occurred, my spiritual life blossomed."

Charlie was curious about Marcus' last comment. "Are you telling us that your spiritual life didn't blossom until you forgave everyone? Haven't you always had a spiritual understanding of life's events?"

Marcus laughed, "No, I haven't always had the spiritual knowledge I now seem to possess. For twenty years of my life I was an agnostic and wasn't even sure there was a God or a spiritual world. Most of the events in my life during those years were very superficial. It was only after I had forgiven all the people I needed to forgive that I developed a spiritual understanding. You see, the act of total forgiveness is a very liberating experience that frees the mind and heart, and allows one to develop spiritually. Greater spiritual awareness and tremendous personal powers are the gifts bestowed upon a person who forgives. Unfortunately, most of the people living on earth will never discover their true spiritual identity and their awesome spiritual powers because they are unwilling to forgive all the people they hold grudges against."

Marcus noticed that the mosquitoes were starting to bite and suggested they return to the dock. He asked, "Would you like to spend the night in my cabin? There are two extra bedrooms and you're welcome to use them."

"Thanks for your kind invitation, Marcus, but would you mind if we just parked our motor home next to your cabin and slept in it overnight? Our beds are already prepared in the motor home."

Marcus thought Charlie's idea was a good one and agreed to it. Marcus started the engine of the pontoon boat and headed towards the dock. He had been so involved in his explanation of the grief process that he hadn't noticed how cold the evening air had become. Marcus offered Val his jacket. She accepted and smiled affectionately as he draped it over her shoulders. Ten minutes later they arrived at the dock.

The day was quickly coming to an end. Marcus and Charlie covered the pontoon boat as Val and Ed prepared for bed. It really wasn't that late, but the day had been so full of activities that everyone was tired.

After having a snack, Marcus and Charlie retired to the front porch. They looked at each other and smiled contentedly. They both knew the day had been perfect. As Charlie sat quietly watching the clouds passing in front of the full moon, he wondered if Loretta's soul was aware that her family was with Marcus. They sat for about ten minutes and then Marcus broke the silence by announcing he was going to bed.

As Marcus stepped through the doorway to his cabin, he looked back towards Charlie and said, "Yes, Charlie, Loretta knows you're here. Her soul has been with us all day. It was her soul that gave me the information I shared with you."

Charlie smiled as tears filled his eyes.

The end

appendix

To My Dying Friend

Did I ever tell you about the two months I spent at summer camp when I was eleven years old? While I was there, I became so involved in the activities that I hardly ever thought about my loving parents and my many friends back home. The camp experience was very beneficial for me and I learned many important lessons about caring and sharing, and even about "puppy love." I remember how sad I was the last week at camp, because I knew that I would soon have to leave my camp friends and return home. Knowing that I would be unhappy about leaving camp, my parents arranged a "welcome home" party for me. As I entered our house, I was greeted by many old friends from the neighborhood. It only took me a few moments to realize how important these people were to me and how much love I felt for each of them. My feelings of love and joy were much more intense than those I had felt at camp. I soon understood that home with my parents and many wonderful friends was where I really belonged.

I tell you this story to help you realize the truth about death and the existence of your real home. You see, you have been so busy with the activities here on earth, that you have forgotten where you have come from. Earth, the place you have been calling home, is not your real home. It's just your "summer camp." It's just one of many teaching facilities that God has established to help souls in their development. Many years ago your soul agreed to visit this facility to learn lessons about love, forgiveness and spiritual trust. The unique life you have been living has been a composite of the many special classes you chose to attend, and now that the classes have been completed, you are about ready to graduate. Your graduation gift from your Spiritual Parent is a return trip home to a Higher Consciousness, to a place some call Heaven. Your Divine Father is aware that you feel unhappy about leaving your classmates behind and, therefore, has prepared a glorious "welcome home" party for you to help you through the transition. At the party you will be greeted by many loving angelic friends and within moments you'll realize that all events occurring within God's universe are perfect and that home in a God Consciousness is where you really belong.

If we were together today, I'm sure you would be asking me to explain death to you in greater detail, so let me list a few additional truths about death.

- *Your soul is in charge of your life and will determine the exact time and place of your transition. Nothing that you'll do will nullify the decisions of your soul.*

- *At the moment of your death, your soul will separate itself from your human body and will leave it behind. It will then travel peacefully through a tunnel of light. At the end of the tunnel your soul will be greeted by many angelic friends and a Supreme Being.*

- *After socializing with your angelic friends, the Supreme Being will lead your soul through a review of life. It's at this point your soul will realize exactly why it was on earth. After the review, your soul will reevaluate itself and then determine when and where in the universe to reincarnate.*

So dear friend, believe what your heart is telling you about death. I'm sure it has told you that human death is not the end of life, so let go of your fear of it, and surrender your human body and earthly worries to your soul. Trust that a compassionate, loving God has designed a "return home" journey for you that is more miraculous than was your own birth. Also trust that Spirit will love and protect those who you'll leave behind. As hard as it may be, please try to enjoy your remaining days at "camp" by filling them with smiles, laughter and love. Think about those people you need to forgive and forgive them, knowing that they did the very best they could under the circumstances. Your forgiveness of others is one of the few things that you'll take home with you.

-Marcus

About the Author

A comparison of Dave Lindsey with Marcus, the fictitious spiritual teacher in this book, would show many similarities. Both are about 50 years old; both were intellectual agnostics for most of their lives; both had a close family member die tragically; both had difficulties forgiving themselves when the deaths occurred; and both had spiritual awakenings shortly after they totally forgave everyone, including themselves.

Dave Lindsey's spiritual awakening came in 1986, fourteen years after his first wife died unexpectedly. At the time of her transition, she was only 28 years old. She left behind a husband and a two year old son. Dave's awakening occurred the day his deceased wife visited him. They talked telepathically for about a minute. Since that day many spiritual events have occurred in his life.

Usually when a spiritual awakening takes place, a person is not only bestowed with a knowledge of the spiritual world, but is also implanted with an insatiable desire to teach spiritual principles to others. Often the person who has the awakening will make major changes in their career and personal life in order to fulfill their calling. Dave Lindsey has done just that. He left his executive position as president of Automotive Technologies, Inc., a technical marketing company, to devote full time to teaching spiritual principles.

In 1990 his first two inspiring books, *Creating a Happier Life* and *Discovering Life's Purpose*, were published. Both books are sold nationally and are quite popular. In 1991 his third book, *Understanding Death and Grief*, was published. Dave anticipates that during the next few years, he will write several more inspirational books about life's mysteries with Marcus as the primary character.

Dave Lindsey is currently the director of the Personal Growth Institute, a Michigan company dedicated to the personal and spiritual growth of individuals. Much of his time is spent giving lectures, conducting workshops and writing books. Some of his thought-provoking lectures are scheduled for prime time television later this year.

The Original Story of Marcus

After reading this simple, illustrated best selling parable by Dave Lindsey, you'll understand why you're living on earth. The story of Marcus' life will also teach you the secrets of forgiveness. Once you understand these secrets, your life will never be the same.

"Discovering Life's Purpose has <u>OUTSOLD</u> every other book in our bookstore during the past 10 months. This beautifully illustrated parable has deeply touched many people in our community."

Ms. Barbara Kruger
Unity Bookstore Manager
Unity of Greater Lansing
Lansing, Michigan

<u>*Discovering Life's Purpose*</u> is a powerful, thought-provoking story that has brought understanding and peace-of-mind to many readers. It's a parable about life...about why we are living on Earth and why we have developed the relationships we have. Once you understand this story, you'll never have difficulty forgiving anyone again.

ISBN: 1-878040-01-4   144 pp, paperback, $8.95

You can be Happier!

Dr. David Lindsey's first best seller contains the keys to happiness. That's why it's so highly recommended.

"I understand why Dr. Bernie Siegel recommends this book to his patients. It's a very inspiring book. In fact, it's currently one of our best sellers."

**Ms. Gloria Phillips, Mgr.
In-The-Know Bookstore
Flint, Michigan**

"I recommend *Creating a Happier Life* for those who are ready to undergo a 'positive' personal transformation. This book will be very helpful in the healing of one's life."

Dr. Bernie S. Siegel, author

THIS BOOK WILL HELP YOU

- •Discover who you really are. •Develop a relationship with God.
- •Understand spiritual laws. •Free your mind through forgiveness.
- •Increase your self-esteem. •Find inner peace through meditation.
- •Discover what makes you really happy. •Develop a happy attitude.

ISBN: 1-878040-00-6   208 pp, paperback, $9.95

WORKSHOP INFORMATION

If you found this book interesting, then you would probably enjoy attending one of Dr. David Lindsey's seminars or workshops. The informative programs are presented in a warm and humorous fashion. For more information, write to:

> Dr. David M. Lindsey
> Personal Growth Institute
> 2638 Browning Avenue
> Lake Orion, Michigan 48360
>
> Phone: (313) 391-1600

BOOKS AND TAPES BY DAVID LINDSEY

BOOKS

- *Creating a Happier Life*
- *Discovering Life's Purpose*
- *Understanding Death & Grief*

TAPES

- *Transcending Life's Illusions*
- *You're More Than Human*
- *Prospering from Spiritual Laws*
- *There's Life After Death*